It's Not Personal,
It's Penis!

REAL MEN FEEL

Lolita A. Kelson

Order this book online at www.trafford.com
or email orders@trafford.com

Most Trafford titles are also available at major online book retailers.

Printed in the United States of America.

ISBN: 978-1-4669-8890-3 (sc)
ISBN: 978-1-4669-8889-7 (hc)
ISBN: 978-1-4669-8654-1 (e)

Library of Congress Control Number: 2013905888

Trafford rev. 04/23/2013

 www.trafford.com

North America & international
toll-free: 1 888 232 4444 (USA & Canada)
phone: 250 383 6864 ♦ fax: 812 355 4082

Contents

It's Not Personal, It's Penis! Real Men Feel, is dedicated to my parents, Thomas E. Kelson Jr. and Hilda E. Kelson, affectionately known as Henry, as well as three men who will remain nameless on the pages of this book. All of you have had an incredible impact on my life.

Daddy—without your loving example, I may not have learned that setbacks are setups for comebacks. Thank you for teaching me that I can overcome all obstacles that inhibit my progress and growth if I look up to God, rise to the occasion, and move beyond temporary defeat Because victory is right around the corner. Thank you, Daddy. (I'll always remember to keep my doors locked and press on.)

Henry—you are my rock, my inspiration, and my number 1 cheerleader. My being blessed to have you as my mother taught me that we do walk by faith, not by sight. Thank you for believing in me when I was struggling to believe in myself, find my own way in this world, and develop into the strong, forward, focused woman, who had you as a role model. Thank you, Henry. (I have grown to know the difference between self-love and selfishness.)

And to the three men who taught me the power of love, the power of forgiveness, and the power of friendship and encouragement beyond measure, all three of you loved me enough to teach me, and no matter how difficult some lessons were—I learned! All three are appreciated, treasured, and valued. And you know it—because I've told you!

To God be the glory for his unyielding greatness, love, and mercy. You are an amazing God, who answers prayers, and I am grateful!

Foreword

LOLITA A. KELSON and I first met while getting pedicures at our favorite nail salon in Baltimore, Maryland. We quickly connected—first, as former New Yorkers and then as two people with a passion for life and an interest in helping to further each other's goals.

Lolita told me about her book and asked for my professional opinion on its content. As a psychotherapist, I work with many men, as well as couples, at my practices in the city of Baltimore and Washington, DC. Over many lively dinner discussions, we reviewed her book's content and conclusions, and I found that they precisely mirror a phenomenon I often see in my counseling practice: the insensitivity that women frequently show to their male partners. This book well illustrates what I know about what hurts men.

Lolita is a daughter, a sister, an aunt, a godmother, a friend, a businessperson, and an author. Her extensive life experiences and acute observations, along with her bold, outgoing interviews with men, make her the perfect author of this book. Men were interviewed wherever they congregated: barbershops, grocery stores, Laundromats, coffeehouses, and countless other locations where she could speak with them either individually or jointly.

Because of her affability, Lolita was able to gain their immediate confidence. Men responded to her questions genuinely and candidly, and this is a key strength of this book. Many women say that they wish their partners would be as open with them.

One evening while dining at a Baltimore restaurant, Lolita and I quickly observed that most men will not respond to certain questions if their wives/partners are present. Readers—whether spouses, partners, or friends—will be able to relate to the messages in *It's Not Personal, It's Penis! Real Men Feel.*

As a wife of thirty years and a mother of sons, I know that men are just as sensitive as women are. As a psychotherapist, I frequently see the scenarios described in the book: the spouses on the down-low, the spouses who engage in emotional affairs in cyberspace, and the women who speak coldly, thoughtlessly, and disrespectfully to their men. I work with clients, using advanced techniques such as eye movement desensitization and reprocessing and the new, innovative modality called brainspotting. By using these methods, my clients and I access attachment wounds and survival terror and begin the process of healing the wounds that cause rifts in their relationships. Good communication must be a key component in a good relationship. Poor communication among couples leads to misunderstandings, which leads to unnecessary relational discord. *It's Not Personal, It's Penis!* is a thorough guide that couples can use to improve their communication style and skill.

As a therapist, I envision using this book as an instructional tool for my clients. It will allow men permission to acknowledge their real emotions instead of the macho exteriors many adopt, either because of what society dictates or the lack of understanding of their inner selves. This book will also be helpful for men returning from war by helping them to normalize the myriad of emotions that are particular to them because of PTSD and other emotional stresses they may have. For couples planning to get married, the book illustrates mores of behavior. *It's Not Personal, It's Penis!Real Men Feel* is a triumph. It is primarily about love and helps people see how they can be more loving toward one another. This book about men is a must-read not only for men but also for those who love them. Everyone will love this delicious book!

Enjoy *It's Not Personal, It's Penis!*

Elizabeth Handy, MS, LCPC, EMDR-C, Brainspotting-C
Baltimore, MD 21224

Acknowledgments

W HILE RESEARCHING FOR this book, I've talked with men from all walks of life, all races, and varied age levels. Most of the men attended either group discussions or individual sessions, which revealed how they felt about relationships with women. I quickly noticed how all the men opened up when they felt comfortable enough to talk about love, friendships with women, and even personal life-changing situations such as bad breakups, necessary losses, and coping with intimacy while experiencing erectile dysfunction.

The more questions asked of these men, the more stories I heard—the more I listened, the more I learned. It is my hope that both women and men will listen and learn from the following chapters, perhaps even creating discussion groups after reading *It's Not Personal, It's Penis!Real Men Feel.* My heartfelt thanks go to all the men who allowed me to question them and contributed to the contents of this book. Indeed, I've learned a lot more than I ever expected because men placed me in a position to listen. Ultimately, I've grown as a woman, I've learned to hear a man's story without debate, and I am more appreciative of a man's presence in my life.

May your life be touched as well!

Introduction

As I sit in front of the chapel on the campus of Morgan State University, my memory takes me back to the days when I walked the campus (otherwise known as the yard), meeting new people and developing life-long relationships. Many of those relationships and friendships were with young men seeking to find themselves while being challenged to understand the women who shared their space at the time. These women, some of them, were confused by the way some men communicated or did not, loved them or could not, and expressed their needs, wants, and desires or chose not to. Plenty of time has passed since those days at Morgan State University. With time comes wisdom and knowledge. Some things change, and some things remain the same. It's a new day, a new culture, yet some of the same issues and concerns that surrounded relationships well over thirty years ago still exist today.

What do men want from their relationships with women? What is it that men try to tell women without speaking the words? Which words would they choose if they only had the forum to speak freely and openly—the platform to share those needs, wants, and deep desires with their female friends, significant others, and wives? Have we really given our men the opportunity to express those concerns and deep desires? Do we really listen when their hearts speak to us? And most importantly, have we provided them with positive answers supported by timely action? We need to listen, we need to act, and we need to hear what our men are saying.

If he tells you he loves home-cooked meals from time to time, then why do you microwave everything? If he tells you he'd like your company on a Friday night because he feels time is impoverished and a little neglected, why is your reply "Sorry, I'm spending time with my girlfriends" or "I have a meeting on Friday night"? And when he's feeling romantic and tells you, why do you gloss over his request with "Maybe another time, I have too much to do right now"? Men have quiet desires that are screaming for attention.

Listen and learn. Let these men speak, let them emote, let them heal—*let them love.*

Chapter 1

He Hurts When

SOME PEOPLE THINK men don't have feelings they're willing to express. What hurts a man's feelings usually stays within his soul. What types of behavior or statements from women or those who associate with a man disappoint and hurt? You may be surprised as you read and learn. It's been said that it's easy to bruise a man's ego.

He Hurts When

- you talk about a former boyfriend while smiling from ear to ear;
- he patiently waits for you to have sex with him, and you say you will, tease him, but have no intentions of going all the way;
- he loves you, shows you, but never tells you until it's too late—he's lost you;
- he cries in the dark, and you don't hold him;
- You always make money an issue because you earn more and you never let him forget it
- he no longer sees a glimmer in your eyes when he walks into the room;
- he knows that you are betraying him, and he suffers silently;
- you compare him to your father or pastor;
- he feels God is far away from him and doesn't even hear his prayers.

He hurts when

- he realizes he's ruined the best relationship he ever had and cannot go back in time to reconnect with his faithful, loyal, loving lady;
- he realizes you no longer have his back;
- he loves you but should not have married you;
- he married you but never loved you
- he breaks your heart and cannot mend it;
- his body is aging and he misses his youthful days.
- he needs the feel of your body next to his, and you turn your back toward him;
- your loved one dies, and he can't heal your pain;

- you are angry, and you throw your engagement ring at him;
- He can no longer carry his weight in the relationship or marriage.
- you shut down on him, and the silent treatment lasts for days.

He hurts when

- you use sex as a weapon against him—as a reward or punishment;
- he thinks you gave him the best years of your life—with regrets on your part;
- he reaches over to touch you, and your body tightens, sending messages of "not now, please go away";
- you tell him "I'm pregnant," and he really doesn't want the baby;
- his past mistakes catch up with his present situation, and you can help him—but you don't;
- he loves and cares about you, but struggles with his sexuality—he's on the down-low.
- you miscarry his baby;
- his career is over or has not begun, and he cannot take care of you or his family.

He hurts when

- his best friend hurts;
- he hears you say "I don't need him";
- he can't understand or read your moods;
- you question everything he says;
- he feels disrespected;
- the weight of the world is on his shoulders;

- you used to take good care of yourself, paying attention to details, and you stop;
- you forget his birthday.
- The empty nest creates anxiety for him and his relationship with you.

He hurts when

- you were a good girlfriend but never transitioned to being a mother and a wife;
- you don't let him be "the Man";
- he shares his secrets with you, and you share them with your girlfriends;
- you tell him to get out and leave his own home;
- you don't spend quality time with him;
- you don't even *try* to love his children;
- he finds out that you aborted a baby of his and never even told him you were pregnant;
- you ask him for the truth, but you can't handle the truth.

He hurts when

- you break up with him, and you start dating his best friend;
- you don't catch him when he falls; you don't even prop him up in his time of need;
- you stop encouraging him with positive affirmations;
- your relationship fails;
- you don't understand that he needs his space—his buddies, nights out with the boys, and his man cave;
- you revisit old stuff that has nothing to do with current situations;

- you leave, and he knows that you are never coming back;
- he gets mixed messages from you;
- he wants children, and as a couple, you have trouble conceiving.

He hurts when

- you hide behind cosmetics, and he admires your natural beauty;
- he feels that you sold him a bill of goods;
- you are his date at a party, and you dance with every man who asks you for a dance;
- you always put your children first, and he feels last on your list;
- he strikes you and realizes he could easily do it again;
- he sees his lady cry;
- he realizes he doesn't love you anymore but cannot walk away.

He hurts when

- his partner, his lover, has become his roommate;
- you don't realize the sacrifices he's made for the good of the relationship;
- he doesn't have your undivided attention—due to your cell phone going off all night long;
- you drove him away, and now, his body is with you, but his mind is on the other side of town;
- someone else got pregnant—before he met you;
- your addictions are destroying the relationship;
- his wife has Alzheimer's, and her world no longer includes him;
- his dreams are fading away, and you don't understand.

- He is sick and realizes his life dreams may not come to fruition
- You constantly remind him of his failures

He hurts when

- your insecurities are too heavy for him to bear;
- you don't realize that he can't bear your pain and you can't borrow his strength;
- you say you forgive him, but you really don't;
- he accepts your mental illness, yet you discontinue your medication and your behavior causes problems in the relationship;
- you commit emotional and spiritual suicide due to being hurt in your past, and you don't even try to move on;
- he knows you're only with him because of his prestige, finances, reputation, and the car he drives;
- you totally ignore him and embarrass him after a mutual breakup.

He hurts when

- he realizes he left the relationship too soon or stayed too long;
- he stays in the relationship with you but does not forgive you, as he said.
- the mother of his child speaks negatively about him while in his company;
- he realizes you never loved him;
- you tell lies unnecessarily;
- you need medication or therapy and stop both, only to find out that your behavior is destroying those who love you;

- he thinks about years gone by when he encouraged your abortions, and now he has children and a family and you don't.
- You don't carry your weight
- You give up on yourself
- You give up on him

He hurts when

- the girl of his dreams ends up being his worse nightmare.
- you know he is a man of the cloth, but forget he is a man.
- you yell at him.
- you can not control your temper.

He hurts when

- you don't realize that some things are better left unsaid;
- you love him for one or two things, and when they are gone—so are you;
- he feels used;
- you hit him, humiliate him, and beat him down with your negative words;
- you die;
- you commit emotional or physical adultery;
- he said he *does*, he *did*, but he *doesn't* anymore.

Chapter 2

He Loves It When

WANT TO MAKE a man feel happy, special, and content? It really doesn't take much, and the results you will reap are worth it! If you're a good listener, a man will tell you . . .

He Loves It When

- he walks into the room and sees a smile on your face when he glances at you;
- you prepare his favorite meal;
- you stop the unnecessary nagging;
- you trust him;
- you are happy;
- he knows you have his back;
- you take good care of yourself;
- you pamper him when he's under the weather.

He loves it when

- he can be the king of the castle;
- you continue to grow and develop your skills;
- you take interest in his interests;
- you don't push marriage too soon;
- you are honest and tactful;
- you encourage dreams;
- you take initiative toward his well-being;
- you understand that he wants you to be the best you can be
- you pray with or for him.
- you are consistent.

He loves it when

- he finds out you are having a baby, and it's the right time in your lives.
- you have faith in him;
- your expectations are realistic;
- you accept his compliments with grace

- you can enjoy family;
- you chase your own dreams;
- you have good housekeeping skills;
- he lays his head on your breasts;
- you cuddle.

He loves it when

- you understand his libido is low;
- there's peace at home;
- you are a good mother;
- you encourage his children and have a positive influence on them;
- you miss him and show him;
- you are confident;
- you support his decisions;
- you compliment him without expecting one in return
- you trust his judgment.

He loves it when

- he trusts you to not go read his text messages or e-mails when he's not looking;
- he's out on the town and other men notice your beauty.
- you allow him to be a gentleman;
- you give him the best you have to offer;
- you surprise him with a gift;
- he feels appreciated;
- you share fun times together;
- you compliment other women—he knows you are confident with yourself.

He loves it when

- you smell good;
- you are sexy and feminine;
- you trust him with your deepest thoughts and secrets;
- you hold his hand;
- you're intimate but not necessarily sexual;
- you are on time;
- you just want to spend time with him;
- you know how to greet him.

He loves it when

- you are passionate;
- you let your hair down;
- you wear dresses and show off your pretty legs;
- you make him feel like he's the only other person in the world;
- he feels he is a priority in your life;
- you truly forgive him;
- your love for God is apparent;
- you smile for no reason at all, and you're happy and content in that moment with no expectations or desires;
- you give him a full-body massage.

He loves it when

- you rub his feet and tell him everything is going to be all right;
- you can watch a sunset and appreciate nature at its finest;
- you share quiet moments together;

- you don't compare him to your ex, father, or brother because you know he is unique;
- your girl talk stays with the girls;
- you whisper a secret, seductive message into his ear;
- you initiate sex;
- you allow him to admire your nakedness.

He loves it when

- you flirt with him;
- you wear different hats—girlfriend, good girl / bad girl;
- you have a sense of humor;
- you wash his back;
- you can teach him a thing or two behind closed doors
- you give him two tickets to his favorite sporting event and tell him to take a buddy of his;
- you realize that he is not a mind reader
- he knows he is the object of your desire in a crowded room;
- you leave love notes—for his eyes only;
- you wink at him from across the room.

He loves it when

- you call him handsome on a regular basis;
- you care;
- you give him his space;
- you speak your mind—not in circles;
- you pick up the tab once in a while;
- you surprise him and order "the fight";
- you let him know you desire, want, and need him;
- you affirm his accomplishments.

He Loves it when

- He can let his guard down with you
- his back is against the wall, and you provide relief;
- you let him finish his thoughts without interrupting him;
- you are spontaneous you leave your bad day at work; you do not carry it home with you;
- you cheer on his favorite team—with him;
- you keep the relationship fresh and exciting;
- you consider his feelings;
- you apologize with sincerity
- you stroke his ego;
- you make good, prudent decisions.

He loves it when

- you read; and you keep abreast of current events -
- you put his request into practice;
- he can sniff your scent;
- you do not cover up;
- you sleep in the nude;
- you don't crowd his space;
- he sees you enter a room with grace and style;
- you respect your parents.
- You understand how much he loves his parents

He loves it when

- you feel comfortable enough to let your guard down and be able to cry in front of him;
- you don't ask a million questions;
- he knows you take time to search for the right card, with the right message to send him;

- you take time to learn him;
- you let him love you;
- he can teach you something; behind closed doors
- your naked breasts lean on his nude back as you sleep together;
- you're vulnerable.

He loves it when

- he knows you are his;
- he's proud of you;
- he marries the right woman for the right reasons;
- you don't rush him;
- you know he loves you—without a doubt!

Chapter 3

Can You Handle It?
A Relationship

MEN AND WOMEN may dream about it, making plans to create it, treasure it, and keep it. When the rubber hits the road . . .

Can You Handle It?

Ever since the women's movement, women's liberation, and burning bras, women have become more independent, verbal/vocal, and competitive. There's absolutely nothing wrong with women being liberated—even earning the same wages that a man would in the same job.

How has the movement affected a woman's role in a relationship with a man—her man? Do women like being in a position to be told what to do by her man? How about assuming a submissive role—not the backseat—just submissive? What does submissive mean to women—to you? Think about this, if you are in a relationship with the man you have chosen to share your life with, haven't you given him permission to have your best interest at heart? If that is the case, then you need to trust him enough to make prudent decisions for you from time to time. And if you disagree, disagree with respect. Follow his lead because he is quite capable. After all, you selected him. Remember, if he really has your best interest at heart, he will not set out to bring you hurt, harm, or danger. You being misguided or misdirected is not in his best interest. If he loves you, cares about you, and respects you, *trust him!*

Can you handle not being able to be Miss Social Butterfly all the time? Can you stay home sometimes—just for the mere fact of being there? Can your needs be secondary once in a while without resenting it and taking it out on your man? And can you really compromise? Do you really want to compromise? When you are in a relationship, you are still independent, smart, and capable of making your own decisions. The one thing you're not is *single*, or *single-minded*. There's a man sharing your space, involved in your territory—a *man* who may not always understand you, console you, and comfort your every desire; a *man* who loves you to be happy but is limited in *making you happy. You,* man or woman, are responsible for your own happiness. Others can only add to what already exists. Can you handle the moods of another person in your space? Does it matter to you if he's talkative today and reclusive the next? Can you handle a relationship with someone other than yourself? Can you handle feeling alone in a relationship with a man or feeling crowded when you crave your own space? Can you really handle what you think you want to, only to find out the reality that you may not handle well or at all!

Chapter 4

Be Yourself, Don't Pretend

DO YOU LIKE phony people? Not too many of us do. So please . . .

Be Yourself, Don't Pretend

How would you respond if you were dating a man who told you he loved to cook—to bake, even—and after dating, being engaged, and getting married, you realized, he told you that, but he actually couldn't cook at all. He couldn't boil an egg without supervision! You'd probably feel a little disappointed and deceived. You may even respond in anger.

Now, flip the script. The man you date thinks you enjoy sports, especially football. Every Sunday, the two of you watch *all* the games together—beginning around one in the afternoon and ending somewhere after 10:00 p.m. Long day, right? But you love football—or at least you told him that. The truth of the matter is, you despise sports, especially football. You simply cannot understand why it takes three hours to play a game that should be over in one. Usually, when a man is attracted to a woman, he's attracted to what he sees, what he hears her say, and the interests they share. When a man is sold a bill of goods and is hoodwinked into a relationship that is based on untruths, he resents it. After all, wouldn't you?

It's very important to men that you are who you say you are. The moral of the matter is simple—be yourself; don't pretend to be someone you have no business being or don't even like. When a man wants and desires to be with you, he's made that decision based on the real deal. Be the real deal, and he won't break the deal!

Go back to the first paragraph. The question was, "How would you respond if you were dating a man who, for the most part, sold you a bill of goods?" not "How would you feel?" In most cases, a woman would respond by ending the relationship. Don't be shocked when and if he does the same. Remember, the truth will be revealed at some point during the relationship, so do yourself a favor and reveal who you are earlier. One, it pays off in the long run.

Chapter 5

You Get Change for a Dollar, Not from a Man: He Is Who He Is

ARE YOU GUILTY of trying to change your man or partner? Well, when you try to change someone other than yourself, remember . . .

You Get Change for a Dollar, Not from a Man: He Is Who He Is

If you don't like the program you are watching on TV, you can change the channel to another. Women have the luxury of changing their look when it's convenient; we change the length of our hair, the color of our nail polish, and even the color of our eyes. If we grow tired of something or grow bored, we make a change. If we see a flaw in our relationship, we may change the relationship or change the man. _Wrong!_ You get change for a dollar, not from a man; he is who he is.

Even though most women know better, some women think they are all-powerful, all-knowing, and so controlling that they can change a man. The man you meet and see is the man he is. If he dresses, lacking a concern for fashion, that's who he is. He doesn't care how he looks. If you go to dinner and he eats with his fingers, that's what he's used to, no table manners. If you are an avid reader and he hasn't opened a book since high school, don't expect him to spend the day in the library with you conducting research. When you share intimate moments together and you feel you're making love to a rock, he just may be emotionally detached—you think? So what do you do? Help him open up emotionally, schedule appointments with a therapist for him, or give him self-help books to help him _change_? If you have any sense, you accept him for who he is, or you walk.

Men cannot change because you think it's best for them. People are who they are, and the only person who you can change is yourself. And quite frankly, most of the men interviewed do not want to change who they are because of a woman's demands. Some men understand that women have the innate ability to influence their significant other. But to remake a man, shape an adult, or remove character flaws is impossible. Ladies, the bottom line is, he is who he is. What you see is what you get, and you can't plant tomato seeds and grow apples. If you want to change someone, change yourself, and you may attract the man you want and need in life.

Chapter 6

He Means What He Says, What Do You Hear?

H AVE YOU HEARD the old saying, "You shouldn't put words in someone else's mouth"? Honestly . . .

He Means What He Says, What Do You Hear?

Unlike some women, men usually are very specific and deliberate in telling a woman what he means. Sometimes he feels confused, and a man will even tell you he feels confused when he feels that way.

Unlike most women, when you ask a man a yes-or-no question, his answer will be yes or no—rarely with an explanation. Here's an example: If a man is asked, "Do you want meat loaf for dinner tonight?" and he answers no, it means just that—no, he doesn't want to eat meat loaf for dinner tonight. It does not mean nor did he say he doesn't like your meat loaf, he's tired of meat loaf, or he doesn't eat meat loaf any longer. He simply means no. So, ladies, what do you hear when he says no? What would your response be when he answers no?

Another example is a woman dating a man and feels curious enough to ask him a loaded question—"Do you love me?" Expect a man's answer to be as honest as it can be at the time of questioning. Since a man could be likely to feel as though he's on the hot seat after being asked that question, his response may sound like "I don't quite know how I feel yet, let's get to know each other better, and perhaps I can answer that question more accurately." He may even say, "I care a lot about you—let's see where this relationship takes us."

OK, so what do you hear, ladies? How do you feel about his response if it's not exactly what you were counting on hearing? Will you take that answer at face value? Although some men may not feel pressured by certain questions, a fair amount of men would rather women allow them time to define their feelings and then willingly share them with women—on their timetable.

It does not hurt to ask men questions; it only hurts when you anticipate the answer but don't hear it!

Men really do say what they mean at the time it's said. And as a sidebar, if a man tells you he loves you, he hasn't said he'd feel that way forever, or that doesn't mean start planning a wedding. He just said he loves you! So enjoy the ride and pay special attention to his behavior toward you—not just those three words.

Remember, when you ask a man a question, be prepared for HIS answer.

Chapter 7

His Man Cave: Peace, Be Still

IS IT REALLY necessary?

His Man Cave: Peace, Be Still

Do you know the satisfaction of being alone in a space of your own and having a sense of peace that only comes from within? Being able to listen to an old song that takes you back to days past when you didn't have a care in the world?

Well, men have described a man cave to be just that—a place of solitude where they can disconnect from problems, people, serious life distractions, and all realities they choose to shelf for the time being.

A man cave is a place where a man can be himself—his total self without being judged or provoked to do something he'd rather not and just cool out. Now there are some rules to follow when a man visits the cave. The top are the following:

- Don't bother or annoy him.
- Be quiet around him.
- If you have to, you *must* enter the man cave for a spell. Be there for a short time, and don't bring any heavy or serious discussions with you.
- And most importantly—it's his man cave, so don't disrupt, disturb, or move anything in the man cave.
- Need less to say, never snoop around his man cave when he is not there.

Remember, the man cave is his and a reflection of what he's thinking about, what his intentions are, and how he plans to relax and enjoy his space for a while. It's a place of nothingness—if that's what he chooses it to be. Literally, a man is doing nothing, on purpose. He is escaping from the cares of the day, the bills, his job, and any defined area of pressure. It's his place of peace for as long as he feels comfortable there. Yes, the man cave is ever so real and necessary. It's also effective, so respect the cave; respect the man.

Chapter 8

Men Pause: It's Menopause

THERE'S A TIME for everything under the sun, a season for it all. During this season . . .

Men Pause: It's Menopause

Have you been feeling a little out of sorts lately? Irritable, anxious, perhaps fatigued during the day? Do you have trouble focusing? Does your mind feel cloudy? Are there thoughts that trouble you? How about loss of memory? Do you remember walking into a room, standing in the middle of the floor, and wondering why you are there, let alone what you came to get? And sex, forget about it! You have no interest at all.

Well, it sounds like the "change of life" is calling. And how do men feel and react to this period in your life? (Actually, there are no more periods in your life.) Although some men recognize the change of life, most men say to themselves, "OK, change already—change back to the woman I know and love!" If you think menopause is difficult for you to handle, what about the man in your life, or the man who used to be in your life, until your crazy mood swings and insecurities chased him out the door?

Most of the men who talked about how they felt about women's change expressed a strong desire to be as understanding as possible—acquiescing to sheets being kicked off in the middle of the night, say ten times or more. Men try to cope with women by treading lightly, staying away from you when you have uncontrolled tantrums or rage out of control for something as small as dropping a pen on the floor. But when it comes to sex and repeated rejection, some men—most men—have a problem with that. One man shared a story.

He said that it was a cold winter's night, and his wife hadn't responded to his advances in over three weeks. He was feeling a little blue about it but did not share that with her—*yet!* Around two o'clock in the morning, his wife left the bed for the bathroom. And when she returned, she was naked. The man immediately felt overjoyed and said to himself, "Wow, I'm going get lucky." To his dismay, when he leaned over to touch his wife and pull her closer to him, she shouted, "I did not remove my clothes for you! As hot as my body feels, please move over because I can't take your body heat as well as my own." She wasn't smiling when she spoke those words either. The man said he felt disappointed, set aside, and even sad—sad to think that his wife no longer found him desirable, sad to think that sex was a memory now, and sad to think that his wife had become a stranger in the bedroom. What used to be a time he looked forward to has become a time filled with frustration and concern—concern that the wife he loved and desired was long gone, never to be found again.

If his wife only knew how she hurt her husband, she probably would have chosen a different tone of voice and perhaps treated him with more care. A woman cannot expect a man to understand her moods, what she is feeling or not, without explaining it to him. All the men who participated in this area of discussion voiced their opinion with conviction. The men would feel better if only their spouse, partner, and significant other would make every attempt to feel better about themselves, whether it's through exercise, change in diet, or therapy to take the edge off. A woman may no longer feel desirable, and her libido may be low or nonexistent; however, the man she's with still has an interest in her, is attracted to her, and has needs he wants met. Ladies, do not make the mistake of shutting down, shutting off, and isolating yourself. Do *all* that's necessary to feel better and behave better. Talk to the man in your life; communicate how you feel and what you need from him. Men say trusting them with the ability to care and understand is paramount to this season in a woman's life.

All seasons change, and we react accordingly; give your man a chance to understand and walk through this season with as much grace as possible. Do not make the mistake of forcing him away because you may end up looking for him—and he's nowhere to be found! It's not that he wants a younger woman to replace you. He may just want the younger woman in you to resurface again! And if truth be told, so do you! So find her, create her, and recreate her to your liking, and everyone around you will feel better—especially you.

Chapter 9

Is It Real? Cybersex

I'VE BEEN TOLD nothing compares to the real thing. Now ask yourself, ask your man, ask your partner.

Is It Real? Cybersex

Back in the day, it was *Playboy* magazine, strip clubs, and an occasional bachelor party that kept a man's attention for a while—nothing too heavy or threatening. Now fast-forward to 2013. Oh my, we have sexting, texting, e-mail, Internet, Facebook, and other social media that can occupy one's company. All these forms of communication are engaging and inviting and perhaps even satisfying. But is it real? Is it harmful? Can it damage a relationship between couples with a healthy intimate life? Is it really fantasy, or are these behaviors used as a method to distract a man's displeasure with his partner? In other words, the one you're with won't, so find someone who will. Is it real, or is it in a man's mind? His thoughts—can those thoughts consume him, perhaps causing him to dismiss himself from the *real* bedroom during the middle of the night while his mate is sleeping quietly?

> Listen to this story. A young man met and found the love of his life while in College. She was four years younger than he which meant that he was in his senior year when she was still a young, wide-eyed freshman—excited about her impending college experience. The young man she was dating landed a good job upon his graduation and proposed marriage to her on her graduation day, Respectful of her beliefs, this couple agreed to wait until marriage to consummate their love for one another, which was done. After a few years of being happily married to his beautiful wife, the man began to hang out on Friday evenings, after work with his buddies. They would go and grab a bite to eat, drink beer and wine together before stopping by Backstage, which was a

community male hot spot. AND THAT'S WHEN IT ALL STARTED! He engaged in sexual banter with two women, exchanged phone numbers and email addresses and started to communicate regularly, just for fun. This seemingly fun stuff, soon escalated to all of them exerting sexual energy by sexting, email, and lucid verbal exchanges by phone . . . even sending photos of each other on the phones. More and more, the man looked forward to the physical excitement he felt from these encounters, to the point of expecting to hear from them on a daily or nightly basis. He once told a buddy of his that he really enjoyed communicating by text and email about sex. He said it gave him a funny kind of high that he was keeping from his beautiful wife because he feared she would not understand. Afterall, he felt it did not have anything to do with her, or did it?

Cybersex—major question—is it just for fun, is it healthy? Does this mean a man is no longer interested in his chosen partner or lover? Should a woman feel insecure about the whole concept of cybersex? Does she have reason to feel rejected by her lover? Does a man think about what effect it may have on his *real* relationship? And does it really matter to him? All these questions were asked of men—all were answered, in some cases, with blank stares, laughter, smirks, or even switched lips curling to the side. For the most part, men—some men—said, "Cybersex, is it real? Perhaps it's just fun. Just a means for escape to satisfy a fantasy."

But does fun for a man mean pain and suffering for a woman? Is it real, cybersex? Is it necessary, cybersex? Is it natural, cybersex? Or is it harmful? *You decide!*

Chapter 10

_____

When Loving Her Is Killing Him

Is LOVE SUPPOSED to hurt? Sometimes it does . . .

When Loving Her Is Killing Him

He goes to work every day, faces pressure at every turn, and budgets his money for the sake of paying the mortgage on time and keeping food on the table. He glances at you while you're sleeping peacefully and plants a kiss on your cheek—so gently as to not awaken you, yet showing his affection toward you. Sometimes he may just admire you as you take your beauty rest—watching and wondering if you're really pleased with his presence in your life. You see, he has to wonder because you seldom share your feelings with him anymore. He wonders, "What more can I do to prove to her I love her, to keep her happy, to keep her mine?" He loves you and wants you to feel secure. He calls you during the middle of the day just to hear your voice, but you're too busy to just say hello. He reaches for your hand while on the couch, watching a movie together, and you jump up and say, "I need to go to the bathroom," only to escape what you think may lead to sex—unwanted sex—that evening, when really, all he wants is to be close to you—not sex, intimacy.

You can't read his mind, but if you could, his thoughts maybe saying, "If she only knew how I feel. I work hard for her, try to do the right thing, and inside, I'm hurting. I pull up to the driveway and sit in the car for twenty minutes before I go in. I've come to dread opening the front door and seeing what used to be a smile now turned into a frown or grimace when she notices me. I used to feel good inside, knowing how much I was loved by her, and now—she makes my stomach turn when I hear that nagging voice. What happened to her, to me, to us? Yes, I still love her, but it's killing me when I'm disrespected and not appreciated. Has she really taken so much for granted when it comes to me? Does she really think that I owe her instead of me giving freely because I choose to? She probably doesn't even notice that we can be in the same room together for thirty minutes or more, and she never even affectionately touches my arm, shoulder, or reaches for a hug! Heck, she rarely says 'please' or 'thank you' to me anymore. I still love her—I just wonder if she will ever get it or if I'll ever tell her!"

What happens when a man loves you, makes sacrifices for you, compliments you, and adores you, yet you pay him no attention? Don't you notice how often he doesn't smile anymore? Can't you feel his sadness? It's quite heavy. Little things can make a big difference in a relationship. Make a change now. Love him, respect him, and show him; tell him how you feel and how he makes you feel. It will make a difference in your relationship. Are you willing to try?

Chapter 11

He Was Gone before He Left

THE RELATIONSHIP ENDED several months ago. It was over! So why did you hang around for so long when your gut told you . . .

He Was Gone before He Left

The date is July 17, 2007. The couple, Thomas and Cheryl, is as happy as they will ever be. They have been living together for over three years, and Thomas realizes that he is unhappy with the relationship—he no longer desires to be a couple and wants to be *out now!* So Thomas does what men would do—he tells Cheryl about his plans to leave, and the rest is a sequence of events.

August 2007—It's been a month now, and Thomas is still living with Cheryl. However, at each private opportunity, he begins to remove his clothes little by little out of the closet. He packs his shoes in boxes and labels them with tape. Thomas is setting up residence in another apartment. Cheryl notices but remains silent in hopes that her worst nightmare never comes to fruition. Even though Thomas's mood is unhappy and unpredictable, Cheryl and Thomas still sleep together. Thomas makes love to Cheryl on a regular basis—or at least Cheryl thinks its lovemaking.

October 2007—Well, Thomas mentions his unhappiness again to Cheryl—this time telling her that he no longer loves her in the same way he loved her years earlier. Thomas still spends his nights with Cheryl but hardly talks to her during the light hours. He hardly looks at her, barely making eye contact, yet sleeps with her for pleasure. All the while, Cheryl notices the changes in her man's behaviors and suffers silently. When her gut tells her something is wrong, she ignores the message or buries the emotion. After sleeping with Thomas, she rolls over and wipes away the tears that roll down her cheeks. Cheryl feels used, empty, and unfulfilled—you know the feeling!

December 1, 2007—Cheryl announces to Thomas that she needs oral surgery and several wisdom teeth extracted. Thomas decides to stay with Cheryl through the holidays before he moves out. After all, Cheryl needs support, and they are "friends," right? After the surgery, Cheryl develops an infection and is out of work for two weeks. During this time, Thomas is taking care of her, shopping for Christmas, and pampering her. Christmas comes and goes, and Cheryl notices things being different still—down to the detail. Her Christmas card from Thomas were always signed "love you, girl." This year, this Christmas card was signed "always." What is going on here? It's obvious that Thomas was gone—before he left. So why doesn't Cheryl let him go and move on with her life? The messages are clear. Is it really possible for a woman to love her man more than she loves herself?

February 14, 2008, Valentine's Day—Thomas and Cheryl wake up to lovemaking—at least that's what Cheryl considers it to be. They talk a bit before leaving for work, and Thomas hits her with "Well, baby, this is the end of the road. Tonight is the night I'm moving out. I'll always care about you—you are special to me!" No doubt, Cheryl is devastated. After all, she really didn't see this coming. But if the truth be told, Cheryl felt this coming, just like every woman who has been in this situation—women who can't *see* or *feel!*

After that morning, Cheryl would never be the same. As a matter of fact, by the end of the day, Cheryl would be dead. Cheryl committed suicide on that most memorable Valentine's Day. While Thomas was looking forward to a new life ahead, Cheryl was ending hers.

The letter she left behind explains a little—but not all:

My Dearest Thomas,

If you are reading this letter, it means that you've found my body on this bed—lifeless, loveless, and empty. My only hope is that GOD will forgive me for being the second person to take my life—you were the first! This morning when you decided to start a new life without me, I decided to end mine. I love you Thomas with every fiber of my being—but sometimes love is not enough. We've shared over ten years together and the only day I regret is the day I realized that you were really gone, before you left me. I saw the signs, I felt the pain of you drifting away. I stood by and waited for the moment when you were man enough to tell me that you were really leaving because I wasn't woman enough to let you go.

Please tell my mother and daughters to only blame me for my demise—not you, Thomas. Tell them I lost myself to you, my identity, myself worth and my reason for living on earth. Tell them when the essence of my soul and spirit melted into yours, I lost my purpose, my reason for living. Tell them to be strong and remember that I will always love them. Please tell them to remember me with a smiling face. I'm so sorry that it had to end this way but I felt my life was over this morning so why wait on time and space to dictate the inevitable—DEATH.

Lastly, tell my girls to be strong and focused—to love themselves more than they love any other. Tell them to keep GOD close and stay faithful to their purpose. Thomas, tell them when a man wants to leave—let him go before it's too late for them to dream again. Tell them I love them, just not enough to stick around—after all, your love for me wasn't enough for you to stay with me. I'm sorry—sorry for the pain. Goodbye, my dearest Thomas.

—Cheryl

Four days later, Thomas attended Cheryl's home-going service at her family's church, where he was welcomed with open arms. The family told him not to blame himself for Cheryl's suicide because they didn't. While at the service, Thomas remembered all the good times that he and Cheryl shared together. Thomas will always remember her with love and fondness; however, he finally admitted to himself that he was gone before he left. When Thomas initially announced his feelings of separation from Cheryl, it was on July 17, 2007—the seventh month and the seventeenth day of the 2,007th year. We all know that seven is the year of completion.

Chapter 12

If I'm The One, Why is He With Her?

Y OU KNOW YOU were a keeper, special in every way. He even told you so. You just do not understand.

If I'm The One, Why is He With Her?

Do you remember dating the man of your dreams, trusting him with your darkest, well kept secrets, sharing special moments and quality time together? Perhaps he was, "Your First". You may have felt complete while in his presence and empty without him. Did he ever tell you that you were the one for him? Telling you he loved you—you were his best friend and the woman he most admired next to his mother or grandmother. He really was in love with you, admired your independence and your drive for success. You really knew how much he cared when the two of you broke up for a while and he came over to see you with tears in his eyes and a tremble in his voice when he wanted you back because he missed you so much.—You believed him, took him back, and realized to what degree, he meant to you as well.

Shortly after that, he told you about the plans he had for the two of you. You met and spent time with his family and close friends frequently, planned trips and vacations together, and even talked about raising a family one day. And guess what? He even told his best friend how special you were. Yes, this man said and felt that you were a keeper—that you were good for him. He seemed happy and excited to spend time dating you and planning a future together. He did everything within his power to please you. Remember the expensive tennis bracelet he bought for you for your birthday—the exact one you picked out while shopping one day? If he was honest and sincere when he told you that you were the best thing that ever happened to him, then why did he drift away, break up with you and end up in the arms of another who, on her best day cannot be compared to you? Was this man too cowardly to tell you that he no longer wanted to be with you, had he outgrown the relationship? Men, some men find it very difficult to tell a woman that it's over.

Some men show you they don't care any longer in hopes of you being the one to figure it out and ultimately make the decision to leave the relationship. Perhaps some men think they are doing you a favor by creating less pain for you. Either way, NO ONE likes to have a broken heart or cause another's heart to break. The same man who told you how special you were, how good you were for him and felt you were the one for him is the same man who knew in his mind, heart, soul, and spirit that he was not the one for you!—And that is the reason why he is not with you and he's with her.—Trust this, it just may be a blessing that he's gone because now you can focus on meeting the one for you while being his one and only. Honestly, when you look back on days gone by—you'll come to grips in knowing that the best is yet to come so move on with your **intelligent, beautiful, and ever so confident self.—He really was not the one—for you anyway!**

Chapter 13

What Now?

*I*T'S *NOT* PERSONAL, *It's* Penis! has been quite a journey with lessons to be learned. You may be left with questions, answers, or even more concerns that lie ahead. No doubt, most of us will walk away feeling some type of emotion.

Are you angry, resentful, or happy to have learned some insights about men and how they feel? Do you walk away, saying, "What about me and how I feel?" Well, those are valid feelings to have, I guess. When the rubber hits the road, we all have to admit it's not always about us—or it shouldn't be! So from now on, consider giving a man the opportunity to express his feelings—and be sure to *really* listen when he speaks. You may be surprised to learn *it's not personal, it's penis*—because *real men feel*.